split the lark

Sue Davies

Oversteps Books

First published in 2021 by

Oversteps Books Ltd
6 Halwell House
South Pool
Nr Kingsbridge
Devon
TQ7 2RX
UK

www.overstepsbooks.com

Printed in Great Britain by imprint digital, Devon

To my family

Acknowledgements

Acknowledgements are due to the following publications in which some of these poems, or versions of them, first appeared: *Agenda, Artemis, Binsted Anthology, Brittle Star, EyeFlash Poetry, Magma, Orbis, Poetry Space, The Interpreter's House, The Wilfred Owen Journal* and *Under the Radar*.

Commended poems are *Oak* and *Ice Breaker* and *Watching my daughter draw a picture in a war zone*. *The Reader* won first prize in the Edward Thomas Fellowship Poets Competition 2020. Other prize-winning poems include: *Caravan, Once, Lords of Misrule, Mango Tree, Flame Eater* and *Stonewalling*. *Free Fall* appeared in *Of Some Importance*, a Grey Hen anthology, celebrating women's contribution to the world.

My heartfelt thanks to all the poets who attend the National Poetry Society's Stanza group in Winchester. The support of fellow poets, their advice, critiques and appreciation have been invaluable. Thank you to the editor of Artemis, the poet Anne Stewart, who has always supported me with her kindness and encouragement. Thank you to Dilys Wood and Second Light poetry courses, the guest poets including Hannah Lowe and Jacqueline Saphra. My warm thanks to Kathryn Bevis, Hampshire Poet Laureate; the poets Patsy Rath, Sue Spiers, and Isabel Rogers both poet and novelist, for their support and appreciative reviews. My thanks and deeply felt gratitude to Alwyn Marriage for her invaluable editorial assistance. Thank you to my family for their support. And very special appreciation to my son, Daniel, whose close readings of these poems have guided me all the way.

Contents

Thaw

Splinter-ice flushes away.
On my mother's lap I listen
to the missed beats of her heart.

A thin string of smoke
casts off like a cat's wail over the firs.
Icicles cloud to a milkiness, drip, drip, drip,

into the snow trough. The roof's red cap
shifts and creaks. In the lean-to
her apples darken and ferment.

And where the axe
dulls in its wood sheaf, there are no strong
hands to break the indolence.

Cycling on Lüneburg Heath

A song sprang out of her. Beneath her red dress
bones like shank buttons studded her back.
She sang quarter notes to the rhythms of jazz,
to the glide of marshland pricked with buttercups,
and the big drum roll of pine and oak.
As we swayed and listed, I gripped the sides
of the child seat, my face with nowhere else
to turn, set against the wind whipping the tops
of junipers. Clouds fell, capped the pines,
and everywhere gems – primroses and foxgloves,
lavender and gorse, the sag and drape of grass.
Her movement pulsed through the metal frame
to my green-stick limbs quivering on the slight incline,
her back bent by the weight of love.

Split the Lark

After Emily Dickinson

Four years old and I could sing in two tongues.
At night in a strange land, I was restless

beneath the earth in the deepest dark among
bone casts of wolves, the purple velvet of moles.

My first language was barred. I whispered
wicked words alone in bed – they were beautiful to me.

To show willing, I practised new sounds like this:
I placed my lips on the silken underside of my wrist,

and with puffs of breath, a pulse in the dip
of my skin, I gave unfamiliar syllables voice.

A gentle lilt of songs filled my head
in the silent wasteland between the forbidden

and the desired. Grandma tried shaking me to life –
Has the cat got your tongue?

My mother called me home. But I was gone.
She wept, afraid I would never speak.

Little Misguided

She kept them in the spare bedroom
on racks behind a curtain with yellow lilies,
the best pairs on top, the shabbiest below.

One of a pair almost mirrored itself –
equal and intimate, like husband and wife.
But I remained alone, without another.

At dressing up time, I lifted the curtain
to pungent leather, fresh from the shoeshine
wooden container to find Cherry Blossom tins

with their little bent unicorn horns,
bearing names of their colour-kin: Oxblood, Navy,
Black and Tan. They lay among spare laces,

soft brushes, and cloths stiff with moon-wax
and spittle. Undeterred by her flat size sevens,
I shuttled them on my bare feet

across the wooden floor like coracles,
shoes for her Puritan purposes –
marching, work and prayer.

Lords of Misrule

Not what I imagined – the woods, dense, untamed
on the tip of Tibbet's Corner where men

were once hanged, swinging south to east. Now
the gilded lambs' tails of hazels, the intoxication

of elder blossom. But our fears outmanoeuvred
the safety of life, home and school,

broke out again by the rope, hoisted over
a hanging branch, the knot tightening

from the weight of boys, smelling of oakum and boats.
But *'they'* were everywhere – their whisperings,

ball-eyed in the scrub. Goose-pimples ran down
our backs as they fixed on us. We kept them

at bay with bravado, screaming as we swung
across the Mere, a grave of strangling weed, rusted trolleys.

As the sun dipped, shadows subdued us. The rope died,
hung heavy and limp. I followed the boys home

along the old Portsmouth Road, toes mulched in mud.
I watched them swagger and joke, pretending

nothing had changed within us,
our pockets alive with frogspawn.

Sly Boots

Safe
in my garden den,
I listened to the wind's
tearing of leaves,
my stripling self
a leaf stalk, feet
curled in socks
like blind moles.
I saw his freckled
upside-down face
begging to crawl
in beside. Each time
he brought offerings –
liquorice bootlaces,
gobstoppers,
lemonade fizz,
and his treat of
super-hero Wonder World
comics.

We soon staked
our frontier,
setting mud traps
covered with sticks,
made up stories – confessed
our fears – drowning
in tangerine
slug slime, or how
giant spiders
might bind us
in their webs
big as spooled floss,
and gobble us up.

Late summer,
our moss skin
thickened,
came unravelled
at the cuffs.
His smooth
lizard tongue
took liberties,
tried entry,
flickered
between my lips.

Cuckoo-dream

I'll always remember our damp little house
on Putney embankment, Sunday bells pealing
to mother's quickness, the tin colander nuzzled
in her lap, her scarred thumbnail shelling peas.

At night, rats scratched my eyelids, sour
river water licked its way along the hall,
slapped the walls, sloshed around our bed legs.
Then let itself out under the back door.

In sunshine, fresh linen in the yard lifted
in the breeze, fragrant with the smell of almond
glue, fine white dust and wood shavings
blown over the wall from busy boathouses.

Swans preened themselves on the slipway
littered with moults of mallards and rose-breasted
pigeons. And when the tide was out, I mudlarked
for clay pipes, porcelain pieces, sharks' teeth.

In Felsham Road, eels knotted and unknotted in tin trays.
The fishmonger's grin, as he winkled cockles
with a pin, came to me in my unwashed sleep,
hunger tasting of dirt and fish, my bed tipping

into morning's tide, the Solent's rough glitter.
Yellow gorse blistered along Haven's cliffs and
reeds whispered to herons and gulls as I lay
pining for home inside the reed warbler's nest.

Wizard

My eyes widen at gleaming nozzles, rows
of syringes, knives and limp white bags like bunting –
not to touch if I'm allowed to attend

the jugglery of his hands, his face bullish,
lips drawn in for concentration as he casts
his spell making me invisible. I watch him

cudgel a fat loaf of marzipan, roll
it flat for each cake's fitting, for the slow,
mouth-watering avalanche of icing

from his tipped bowl, palette knife, a wing
that works the air, then a baton swept crossways
smoothing thermals, nicks of blade levelled

like driven snow. Brow puckered, he pipes
trails of white roses, scrolled leaves, arabesques
at the foot of plinths. A stolen pinch of marzipan

warm in my palm, I watch him stack the cakes
clumsily on pillars, the Ice Queen's palace
glowing pearlescent like the moon's cold skull.

Safe from splintered glass, he places
the tiny bride and groom under the bower
on the top tier, his goliath fingers trembling.

The Reader

Harrison Primary School, Fareham, Hants, November 2015

It is so peaceful here ...

through the tall school window, copper oaks
orchestrate the wind.

I listen to their low
percussion of shaken leaves.

Bat boxes are now exposed,
nailed to trunks already wounded
and scored.

         Bethany comes with a book,
         tousled hair and climbs the chair.

         I try small talk, but her mind is set –
         to find both her place and voice.

         Her finger brushes every word,
         her legs scissoring to cadences

and rhythms of distant feet,
marching through flak and mist.

I think of the small brown wren
with a song

so strong
it can send off
the hawk and falcon.

         Suddenly, Bethany stops,
         pins *gently* down by its tail.

         I love that word, she says, and leans into me.

When *gently* lifts from her breath, it flutters
over a stippled meadow of sun-shot poppies,

their heavy seed heads turning in the wind.

Skulduggery

Once the key twisted in the lopsided lock, the lid dropped
to a ledge, and I put my face inside his writing bureau –
for the allure of its lemon-wax lustre, pencil shavings,
walnut veneered shelves. Drawers, too, spilled
their scents, overripe apples, peppery dust. I loved
the feel of paper, velour and tissue, like sepals
closing in on family secrets – their Gothic scripts
of annulments, births and deaths. I disturbed cake crumbs,
pocket fluff in pigeonholes wedged with blue envelopes
addressed to him in a stranger's hand, sophisticated,
more grown up than mine. The letters were tender,
intimate, words taking possession of him. Green-eyed, I took up
his ink pen, tried my signature beside hers, curlicues
like connective skein, our names bleeding into one.

The Dare

Our legs long
as spider crabs', we sat on moss
and straddled the wall that ran the length of our road.

Trespassing without guilt, we stole
peaches, sweet as summer's rain, bronzed
like the toads asleep in crevices weeping salt.

Before, at home we slipped
under our mothers' warnings to keep
clean and crisp, your curls like wood shavings,

and tore free in bare feet, running the wall
from east to west, our feet assured, gripping
ivy and rock cress.

Once, when the sun ignited the limes,
you said I had to jump. My knees
weakened at your command – a law

to which I must submit. We stared down
into the earthen pit. And before
a scream shook from you – I leapt

shot from golden dust to mid-air

my life there
for that moment held ...

and nothing else.

Gift

I have known the inexorable sadness of pencils
Theodore Roethke

You fossick in the dirt with a stub pencil,
your face angry, insolent; then a practised look: *I don't care* –
given detention for doodling.

One hundred lines: I *must not draw in the margin*
hurts your hand and brain. She is lonely, too,
in the empty classroom, the teacher,

now a custodian working at her lookout desk.
You watch her pale wrist shifting across her page,
slow as the hand of the stertorous clock.

You note her neat row of pencils, lined up
on parade, tiny bayonets sharpened for combat.
Scrutinizing her, you suspect that she, too,

finds refuge in margins. And for that
you take up your page of wasted words, fold
a square into diminutive shapes. Your hands

need no prompting. They know the sequence,
symmetry and coupling – the accomplished
conjugation of twists, turns and folds until

finally, your fingers coax to life the wordbird,
speckled wings, a head, tail and beak,
the breastbone firm, strong as a keel for flight.

Caravan
1916

The boy with thick curls lay in its vacancy –
a little oil lamp burning beside the makeshift bed,
shutters closed to the molten eyes of nightfall.

Only the grey mare, witness to dawn, saw him
trip down the steps to the river, tread black water
while swifts switched blades and surface-skimmed.

Then back on the road again, his father's reins
held slack, the milk churn squeaking on its hook,
china and cutlery tinkling to various phrases

of their procession. And not forgetting mother's
burst of sunflowers in the tin jug and her freshly
knifed dash in the panel of wood to mark his summer's

growth, long before the mare was sold to pull gun wagons,
her frozen fetlocks hot with mud fever, the family's
caravan hauled to the Front, stripped by the surgeon's

brutal carpentry, the air peppered with sawed bone.
Stretcher bearers slipped on blood to deliver a wounded man.
Astonished, he caught sight of his notched rise to manhood

in a panel of wood and through a mustard haze,
the shutters closed; the little oil lamp shimmered beside
his makeshift bed, blazed briefly, and died in his eyes.

Flame Eater

His shopping list on the back of a letter takes us
back to a time when the world was motionless –

the sun in earth's sphere crabbed its latitude
like a dog in skirts tottering on its hind legs.

Fairies decked out in mothy wings dance
in the ring, reminding him little Vincenzo

needs slippers and his wife Marina is bound to beg
for new plates to perfect her juggling and spinning.

Pepper, cinnamon, cloves, jams and raisin spelt,
he lists as a matter of urgency for trapeze artists

who leap under the canopy like fleas,
blood spots dancing before his eyes as sunrays

snipe through the pole hole at chained bears
whipped to staccato rhythms of Vincenzo

practising the scales. *Don't lift your fingers, Vincenzo,
slide! And remember the foot pedal!*

In the din of rehearsals, he remembers to order
artillery balls, tin pipes for clowns, not forgetting

a cartload of hay for the horses. *Listen here!
Listen here*, he cries in the ring, tailcoat

trailing sawdust, proof smouldering under his hat.
I've made a discovery to put an end to tyranny!

The sun is fixed in the heavens. It is the earth that spins!
Truth like oxygen fuels flames from Galileo's mouth.

The people rise and applaud, whoop and dance.
The new moon and tides bear witness.

Flight of the Enchanter

It was there we returned breath to air,
snagged by gorse lanced with yellow welts.
Then columns of lace and white-linen flowers
along the sea-green flanks. She held my hand
tight, which stopped my blood, and I was drugged
by her power, the perfume of pine and grass, just
able to lift my feet, knees freshly scabbed,
rickety from city streets. The path was pounded
dead, grey baked clay, where nothing grew –
even hissy dandelions stopped short without
a chance to root. But the light cut our eyes
like diamonds – ferns and nettles glowed
white-gold, birch leaves darted like fish
where the path narrowed and slothed off
into the murk.
        Deeper still, thin saplings
leaned over the fading path, their crowns like puffs
of cloud among oaks cracking their dry
roots above earth. *We're taking the hardest path,*
she said, to *teach you the ways of the forest.*

Listening to Trees

When I was small and sickly   my skinny hands
banded together books by their woodland scent and colour –
gold-crowned wrens robin redbreasts yellowhammers
their sapling spines springy as wild cats.

I stacked sturdier books black raven towers brooding
in dark swamps.   But when I could read   books became
portals to other worlds   and their words   flocked on
the wire singing   and I could listen and dream with ease.

We lived in rooms lined with bookshelves colossal as trees
buckling the brain   as I lay feverish   in the nutty hollow of
                   the settee –
hell's flame in an acorn   flawed moonlight coming at me
like the wicked   pretending to be like   everyone else.

Birches whispered down the chimney   I heard the tinsel
of acers   rasp of ash   my face breaking out in spores
my pod mouth swollen with sycamore seed   and I longed
to scatter a forest of my own   work the old Olivetti   unlock

the mysteries of *qwerty*   strike keys   brass edges perfect
for fingers craving delivery   the carriage return's *ting!*
tap tap tap of the elegant ampersand   the pulse of tree rings
spooling black ink   snarl of levers   my skin peeled clean.

Boarders at Cowan Bridge School

In memory of Maria and Elizabeth Brontë

Too bad their curls had to fall, the pitchers
solid with ice. Hungry and whey-faced
they knelt in prayer, the eternal hour willed
to flash-rabbit across the fields for a cup of milk.

In the classroom, the cane's threat, its brittle back
bowed like their own, bending over chalk and slates.
Afternoons, they took long walks in the famished
mouth of the wind, longing for bread, cloudberries –

not the black hearts of splintered gorse, rancid meat.
Evenings in the candle dusk, they hemmed along
frayed edges of cloth, a desire to lay their feverish
heads among hyacinths slipstitched in cotton grass.

Nights of wracking coughs, night sweats; pining
for home, their spirits danced among junipers,
their wasted arms pinned to their sides, a penny
pressed on each eye, bodies light as siskins.

Propinquity

After Ruth Stone

Suffocating in the hot villa, she drags the mattress
onto the cool veranda, stars make their spider silk,
others cluster like saltlicks in deep space sharing

the same circuitry as white noise, solar flares,
intimacy, the vertigo of radiance. Lying there,
her face to the galaxy, she curses Newton,

Hegel and Kant, praises woman face of the earth,
her business of mind and body doing their work.
She remembers to cover herself because who

could resist her vacant mysteriousness? Lilith
returns to the fold, wild, intelligent, listening
to the slap of small feet along the unlit hall.

They have come to look for her, confident
in the dark as if to lay their eggs in her softest pulp.
They lie close. She feels their boneless delicacy –

limbs fidget and embrace. Jasmine petals
taken by the breeze settle on their damp hair.
She smells apple on their sleeping breath.

Solitary

...life slips by like a field mouse,
not shaking the grass.   Ezra Pound

On the sill, the obdurate woodblock calendar,
the day vanishing: a pink sea-urchin shell
beside a picture postcard, Matisse's
Lithographie sur le Thème 'La Pompadour'.
And beyond, lights in houses, unfaltering
in the sycamore's dark emphasis. What thoughts
I have of you tonight ... translations, dreams,
letters, only words to go by, merchandise hidden
in books; familiar histories; a multitude of rooms.
Your room ... I don't know, shuttered, fastened
against the mistral; the light under your door
says you are home for the night courier,
for a mouse slipping in from the grass.

Pillion Rider

On Lavender Hill he stopped for me –
visor up, astride his bike, a voice
like amber, smoothed against silk.

I was woken from sleep –
a wink of sun, the air depth-charged
set fire to my skin. I was multitudinous

as a beehive and broke the word *No*
in half like a stick. His eyes flashed, head
bowed in mock courtship.

Making a fool of speech, his gloved hand
patted his machine, *C'mon. C'mon!*
I took a chance, and we lifted off.

I pressed myself closer, we leaned as one,
our feet winged, my hair
caught in the stars ...

                              *

My grey hair catches
on winter brambles.
He promised to love me
forever.

I wait. My small bones
grow lovingly inside him.

Little Testament

After Eugenio Montale

Dear Signor Montale,
Forgive me,
I have taken the snail
out of your poem, and now place
it gently into the grass, watch its eye-
stalks melt into muscle, head drawn back,
afraid of salt, and drought; afraid its delicate shell
might be pounded against stone
in the beak of a thrush.

All the same,
I'd like to consider my life
as a snail, contemplate the world
from the underside of a leaf, in a way
a woman can't; woman with her chapped,
ruddled hands and a tongue
stilled in the invisible scold's bridle.

Encompassing
both sexes, I'd cavort in slimelight,
marvel at the peace and economy of my existence –
house and sarcophagus, my beginning
and my end, secure on my back.

I'll listen for the sobbing of bloated rivers,
resurrection of dry stalks
and spring water surging up,
slippery as fish.

And if things
get really tough,
I'll hibernate for decades
behind the dry eye of a tyrant,
rip into his consciousness with my ribbon
tongue and then make my slow return to you
as something essential –
my trail like *diamond-dust sparkle*
flashing hope through your mind
when the light goes out.

Icebreaker

A blue light glows beneath the ice, snow beasts
lumber towards the Thames – *Teme* dark and numinous,
a divinity, a guardian of settlements.

Now, telephone wires are down, the Serpentine's carp
lie frozen, predatory gusts tug on tethers, echo-locate
the house. I watch gas flames make herring

shoal on the wall as you recite *L'Albatros,*
majestic bird, limping on deck, wings dragging, butts
of hoots and jeers, spilling gutweed and lead pellets.

Under rough blankets, our skins stick like snow pills.
There can be no unpicking now. Swallowed whole,
we drift far out into the ocean.

Our hearts slow to leeward edge. In dream sleep, we listen
to the boom and creak of ice floes – your paperbacks safe,
stuffed between ribs, your guitar propped against the dorsal fin.

Free Fall

Consider Sappho shivering in her summer dress.
Bird boned in the glint of the moon's thin blade,
she walks ahead on the cliff path of tender grass.
Like you, she loved pomegranate trees, oleanders made
thick with flowers, watched clouds pass like camels,
padding bare hills of Eressos with cushioned feet.

Despite slander and the warp of time, think well
of her – of her bold, gentle heart, poems to blast
hypocrisy, her belief in love's immortality, wings
clipped never silenced the lark. I take your arm, casually.
Your words, like compass needles, reverberate and sing
through rock, earth's chalk skin, and the rolling sea.
Even the grass grows pale when we dare look down.
You pull back as though you had always known.

Psyche

No, it wasn't a hunter like him – scattering
his bladesmith filings, hammering steel
when the stars didn't know their resting places
and the moon less of her pull –

but a dreamer who sings to herself as she works,
strews pores of the vanilla-scented heliotrope,
spins wild cotton lint, and unfurls
with delicate skill a chrysalis' oak-leafed
silhouette, and paints with a steady hand.
an eye on each thrilled wing.

To finish,
a brush of gold pollen dust for its torso.

Look, how this exquisite
courier of souls, staggers from the box hedge
into the moonlight.

Easter in Nazareth

To Sarah

Pilgrims throng the streets with eggs
boiled in bright dyes, woven crosses of fern
and palm waving, held high.

The convent rises above flat-roofed houses,
built of sombre stone, more a fortress for the pious,
contemplation and repose. At the door

we ask for a room and we're shown a cell:
high-grilled windows, rough, cold walls,
leaden light falling on bare beds and boards.

At supper, nuns assemble at the refectory table,
faces encased in starched cotton, mouths barely
opening and closing on a peck of crumbs.

From a chair on high cushions, your curls in disarray,
you're keen to impress with celebratory spoon and song –
I had a little nut tree ... Old King Cole...

Sunrise, and more turmoil in the courtyard –
shrieks, laughter, clapping of hands, the sun's charity
like a gold coin, flips over the convent wall.

Packed to leave, we lose, then find you. Nuns in white aprons,
skirts hitched, sleeves rolled to their elbows, playing
chase with you in the shadows of the colonnade.

Hex

A night in Cyprus during threats of an imminent Turkish invasion

Calling us awake, the owl lifts off
from the moonlit olive grove.

Eyes barely open, we shoulder-buff
the wall on our way, perhaps as your picture book
suggests, to fill a cauldron with marsh frogs,
worms gently poached.

We set to work: saucepan, syrup, goat's milk,
nectar from the Tantalus jar,
stirred on the blue flame, long spoon held
in your dimpled fist.

The morass pops, seethes
to Aphrodite's foam and settles to a magma crust.

Our faces on the pan's shine mimic
blobfish. We giggle and wobble while the potion
cools and sets.

I slice through the golden wedge.
On our tongues, warm fudge gives up its sweetness.

Oh, how I love your company, safe here
in our honeyed drunkenness, the sugar baby
inside me driving us to the edge of our wits.

Stonewalling

In skeins of dust, I shadowed your
hands like Sisyphus, your body
tense, sinews taught. We hammered
and spliced, thrust and nudged
grit and pebbles into cracks, our
shoulder blades aching, hands raw.
I wanted to touch your tender skin,
your musculature, searching for you,
begrudging sun and moon, the arrival
of spring. In bed we lay like effigies,
the wall naked between us, its stones
bearing down on our blunted tongues.

That summer, toad flax, angel hair,
milkweed seeds blown from fields
fell on barren stones. But the wall
spun a heart around itself, salvaged
moss pulp, lichen skullcaps, fledgling
feathers left in empty nests. The house
nearby shed its ghost bloom to drift
like the stars and the stones turned
blue with the moon's erasure. Then,
our endeavours at an end, you left me
to fend for myself. I let the stacked
topping stones lie idle for years in
wild witchgrass, unforgiving as scars.

Water flea

(For Isabel who asked for something small)

Where did nature find a place in a flea for all the senses?
                              Pliny the Elder, Natural History

She skits and frisks, scintilla
of luminescence,

her black eye-pearl
darting in its marshy scallop.

Close to her heart, a supple
brood-pouch of hatched replicas

throbs in its yokey glob,
while her propeller makes little cloudbanks,

and her fat spike is
at the ready to gore predators.

Mesmerised,
my eyes wobble like twin planets,

watching her upside down
birthing dance, her young

pulsating
along the birth canal, shooting

into the blue spectrum of the water bowl.
They know nothing

of dust devils,
tides, hurricanes, the moon's derangement.

Footloose

To Sophie

I liked to knead your feet before your infant bones coalesced.
But now, padding the flagstones, they're shaped for navigation,
treading the groundswell of Bere Forest, crunching down
on the Solent shore where sanderlings stab the pebbles.

Once, after feeding the horses, we cycled barefoot
along Meon's path, raced through the spooky woods,
and in the garden dropped our bikes to play badminton,
the net imagined, suspended like a trance.

And although the blackbird stopped singing, we couldn't stop –
our bare feet slipping on damp grass to the *ping* and *pock*
in a dream of apples, florescent in phantom blossom,
the shuttlecock's arc aflame in the dusk.

Bone Diviner

You took the night passage, pressed together,
one mass of humanity huddled in an open boat
with nothing to own but your lives.

Did you believe you could fly in the starless sky,
or swim like quicksilver fish? Show men with guns
your empty hands, palms upturned, soft

as belly plates of turtles, moon-yellow,
on which I've written my prophesies.
Tides roll over the hot stones and Nubian dust

crosshatches on clay floors. Remember love songs
scored on wing bones and how fissures scorched by flame
can tell how enslaved you are – how despite the mind's

heft you work asleep, flea beetles underfoot,
treading slack-skinned grapes, their juice
sluiced into a vat that some wretch drowned in.

The sea's deadpan face keeps the secrets of my oracle bones –
when to plant crops, when to feast, and when to fast.
When you should chance the crossing home.

Watching my Daughter Draw a Picture in a War Zone

She's got hold of me, tethered to her blue crayon,
my body an island, its isthmus the cord still attached.

Wings appear, folded back, my spine fastened by knots.
I wonder if before flight I'll rock on my southern hemisphere
blessed with talons instead of feet.

She breathes hard with concentration, curls
her tongue, joining pincer bone to bone,

                             my skull
emptying artillery shells –

boom boom   boom
echoing in the hills of Buffavento.

We listen.

Fear in her blue eyes hurtles into mine –
I smile to mask panic –
                   It's only the explosion of flowers, I say,

knowing gods blanch at the savagery of war,
mass graves without marigolds, poppies, their seed heads
split and miscast.

Calmer now, she draws my face from memory,
a flat patina, soft rut of mouth, eyes pinpoints,
half blind beneath webbed brows.

                      I wait
for a tangle of hair – instead, she draws a halo, a dog fox
inside howling at the murmuration of fighter planes
over Strovolos at dusk.

Later, we're advised to leave, she's quick to save
her unfinished picture from masonry silt.

                              Cat on her lap,
we flee to Akrotiri, the car crashing over potholes.

I picture lemons
rotting on trees, our back door playing dead,
its jaw hinged apart.

Mnemosyne

They taught me how you were once pieced
together according to your nature, your body parts
whole, alive and kicking elsewhere.

Here your uniqueness, taste and touch
are preserved in vials, safe in storage suites.
But as a confessed quantum sceptic

I wonder how a cup of coffee can grow cold
but not grow hot. How a glass can break
but not come together again. And how,

when a child implores *Make it work! Make it work!*
his father looks on, helpless, unable to kick-start
the bumble bee's tiny heart.

I ask how many parts of you labelled
in my folds and fissures I can retrieve –
the smell of your skin, your animal allure

prowling in my subatomic territory, your voice
travelling along my neural threads so that you
stand before me, and unbreak my heart.

Pietà

For Paula Rego

Her red skirt is spread,
Mater Dolorosa – head forced back, throat
goose white against the palette knife
dipped in cinnabar.

He arrived in a jet of blood
where she holds him now,
his body unyielding
as any tree crushed against her.

Most have forgotten how,
as a boy, he carried a rooster home
under his arm.

And later, waved a white rag
in the fire-bombed dusk.

We know what has been stolen from us.
Did you see her lifting her torn skirt,
and climb over rubble to save him?

The Ink Makers
China 23 BC

First, they ensured casements were sheeted
to keep out the autumn wind and the door
draped with fine mesh bulging inward
near the furnace. In winter, they used
cow hides to keep out the snow, ice blue
tracks left by sledges, sheep and lynx.
In summer heat, they tied wet rags over
their mouths to save their throats, took
comfort in fragrances of camphor, cassia
and pine – all the business of ink, together
with glue, turpentine, the lotus flowers
whittled from wood, brandished against
vermin, the spoil of flies; they learned
to measure, grind and stir, pour infusions
into flower sticks without spillage, every drop
precious for poets and philosophers. Never
shown how to read or write, they tattooed
signs inside their wrists for lovers – deaf to old
wives' tales and warnings, poisoned blood,
tongues and lips ink-stained by years of captivity.

Strawberry Thieves

Supper table set, she watches him chop
tomatoes, pips spawning off the blade.

She senses the ending and leads him
to belly along the straw-bedded fields,

lift leaves to pale opals, their seeds amber
as the ring around a blackbird's eye.

Breathing in the distilled scent
of wildflowers, they lower their heads,

close their lips on strawberries, heavy and ripe,
nip stalks, crushing the little hearts

to burst sweetness on the tongue.
When the lookout boy waves his arms

and hollers in protest, they rise,
brush themselves down, turn their backs on him.

Storm clouds ramp over the spruce and lime.
They shiver in the evening rain needling

through the skylight. At the table, she sits
before an empty plate with hairline cracks,

breaks bread, sips wine. He watches her mouth,
awaiting her *Adieu, auf wiedersehen.*

Mango Tree

Close your eyes and tell me if you remember strange fruit –
bodies swinging from poplar trees in a southern breeze
bearing the scent of cotton bloom and magnolias?

Then let me take you by the hand to the mango tree,
its heady blossom spent; evergreen leaves wreathed
over doorways, welcoming home brides, leaves soon

to fade, turn brittle in summer's heat. Come,
sit beside me in your dream. The goddess Ambika
with night blossom in her hair, sings to the full moon;

mango seeds make soft pulpy flesh, and flocks
of sunbirds like flames flash through the canopy,
the lonely hoopoe whistling for her mate.

Can you smell the jasmine perfume in the air,
catch the fragrance of cardamom and temple incense
on the cusp of an uneasy stillness as you imagine

the roar of tigers in the forest? But listen, mothers
are calling for their lost daughters you mistake
for Little Owl's *kakkuo, kakkuo* … and the sly cobra's

puff of dust makes you thirst for water and muskmelon juice.
At dawn, we wake to an aftertaste of decay, the dry,
musty savour of humanity, stench of human waste

dissolving the night scents of flowers, and see
two girls hanging from the mango tree. The earth
quakes open, soaked with blood. Myna birds screech.

The sun rises, ferocious. Cameras flash,
suck at the spectacle – help us take them down.
Be gentle, please, be gentle.

In 2014 two girls, one aged 14 and another aged 15, were repeatedly raped, strangled and strung up in a mango tree in the village of Katra in northern India. It recalled the lynching of African Americans in the southern states of the US and Billie Holiday's song 'Strange Fruit'. The mango tree, and all it represents in Indian culture, was also defiled.

The Sitter

Her coat falls over the chair. She unbuttons her dress.
He is selecting his rags and brushes, tubes of paint.
She sits naked before him, settling herself, hired out,
hands over her pubis, arms pressed on her breasts.

She is not shy, but cold. Yet love stirs. Her heart tips
its blood's worth for him. He says her eyes are blue irises.
But this is business – his mind instructs, dissects,
dislocates – an arm set *here*, legs pulled apart like *so*.

She fears he'll loot her, make a travesty of hardship,
her hidden distress. Her eyes settle on the ceiling's stucco,
salty fern fronds like filets of lace. He doesn't mix colour –
vermilion, sapphire, burnt sienna – mantra on his breath.

He feather paints, frenetic. His gaunt cat fixes its stare.
The sitter dreams of a table set for supper. Coppers
in a bowl dull to verdigris. Later, the small oil
is exhibited in Paris: *Fille avec chat*, her hands unfinished.

Double Take

In memory of Sarah Davies, née James

A loose photo tucked in the dark. I view
their faces as if through a night scope –

great-grandmother Sarah, best apron starched,
a baby on her lap, scowling into the pin hole.

Beside her sits great-grandfather Ted,
tilting forward, fortified by his slate suit,

wing collar and watch-chain luminous
in infra-red light. I'm astonished how

energy still pours from their eyes, and imagine
they're making their way up the path

to the house, raw coal crunching underfoot,
while I search for them in censuses: births,

marriages and deaths. At teatime, she offered
a plate of laver bread with the cramped hand

of a coal hewer, her heart atrophied by grief –
two dead babies, Ted's incurable cough,

and not enough pennies to pay for help.
Her prayers unheard in Merthyr's Fault –

mine explosions, boys with stunted growth,
she defied her Calvinist God, insisting

her three remaining sons abandon picks
and cutters, take up learning, precious books.

In Llwydcoed, she hoisted with pride
the line-prop for all to admire – among threadbare

sheets, white shirts billowed in crosswinds.

The Blue Handkerchief

I left her for a while on a shelter bench,
small-boned, fearless, on the threshold of death.
I hurried back with melting ice-cream, a sense
that looking for me, she might have wandered.

Across the dip in her lap, she'd spread
a fresh handkerchief, her patient, rheumatic hands
lay on the laced square of blue linen, her head
held high to become the country girl again.

We licked ice-cream to the same rhythm, tongues
feeling the cones' rough edge, both thoughtful –
past misgivings, shame and hurt, all our wrongs
a sorrowful, brooding guest between us.

She folded her handkerchief on the lines
of its pressed quarters, as if something precious
lay inside, untouched, kept secret, free of stains.
And tucked it up her sleeve to keep clean.

In the clear sky, a gull wheeled like a flung
wishbone, the sea rocked before us, a gentian
expanse of damselflies; the highly-strung
Spinnaker wind carried wafts of *Blue Grass*.

Siren

Dusk. The sea smoulders with indolence.
The sand, scalloped by bathers, cools and settles.
White houses skitter down the hillside, then
pull back, darken and contract. As light fades,

the tamarisk trees shake off raucous cicadas,
and a stillness commands reverence. Swallows
roost on the wires like prayer beads and the veiled
moon is shy as a young snail under leaf.

From the quay, the swimmer dives in, brawny
arms slicing the black water. My eyes lock
onto his shoulders, their plunge and twist. And though
I'm small in my shoes of pearl, and my blood

is briny and thin, I sing across the dark water
to bring him in, watch him change course
towards the reef. Then, the weaving of stars,
my final tug on his thread and the water's shiver.

Reading *Macbeth*

Will a little water flush away what's been done?
Time tells us the horror grows, and the light has
gone from our days because we have given in
to violent expeditions of love. What has become of us
holding our tongues in stolen afternoons, scorpions
stinging? Once tender as a flower, I now trade in blood,
my eyes forever open, yet unseeing in the murky rain,
driving on the motorway, my heart shot through
so all the salt in the sea won't heal the schism, this body
in need of you, in need of oblivion, a purgative to make
me pure again. There's a knocking at the door. I place
one foot carefully in front of the other, sleep walking
from you awake in the dark, wringing my raw hands
that all the perfume in the world can never sweeten.

Muse

Why must you lay waste to borders, your body's
excesses spilling over its own fracture lines.
I'm here, your faithless stalker, hopeless voyeur.

Your serpentine neck once burst from its cracked seed,
rooted down for sustenance in yourself.
My lips are dry, my breath gasps its censure.

I face you naked, without artifice, because I look
for truth in you: I want to know if carnal thoughts
and depravities spill from your eyes. But through

a thin veil of light, this is all you answer to – bone
jarring on bone, blue-leafed bruises inking the psyche.
With aching hunger, I watch you watch yourself –

duplicitous, as always, the twin repositories
of death and life. How can you love with so much poison
in your heart? Your eyes drill into mine

until a stream of silver folds over you. The bevelled
edge glints, frames the vacancy of your mind.

Quake in Kalives

She craves an apple, so he sets off to market,
striding to the counter beat of cicadas
like the last of the water deities, faint

in a mirage of heat. Done with bees
and finches, sunflowers have dropped their empty heads.
From the back door, she watches the sow

trotting her piglets along the shore
for their morning wallow in the waves –
not for them arabesques of grief, or the longing

for home, for blackberry hedgerows thick
and spidery, the sea's phosphorous rage
against chalk cliffs.

Here, red kites turn, buckle on drifts.
On the table, curdled milk, a bowl of split figs.
Inside her, a life knocks with its little fist.

*

By the lagoon, the gold-splashed ibis,
startled by suddenness, take flight.
Without warning, hammer blows,

fall of masonry, rock and silt –
hauliers shouting, sweating, pulling ropes,
the priest blessing the heaving bulk.

Spume froths around its baptism. The darkness
cool, antediluvian. Cloudy water sucks
her back and back. Then a violent surge

and she is thrown into light, bruised,
a pale heap on the sand to be tended by strangers,
coaxed awake, an apple polished
like copper in his hand.

EX LIBRIS:

Niccolò Machiavelli

Midsummer – worried their spines
might peel from melting glue, their pages
curling in the Florentine heat,

he kept them locked in sequestered gloom,
shutters nailed to frames, drapes drawn,
the sun an incandescence of disgrace.

Unique, rendered mute, rarely chosen
for fear of spoiling, they remained aloof, until
made supple by his hands, their deckle edges

untrimmed: myths, testaments and revelations
sewn inside their signatures; enlivened by the eye,
words lay dormant in his fallow darkness.

Only in candlelight, the key double-turned
in the lock, did he take up his knife and slit open
their uncut pages, a ritual of exquisite pleasure

to subvert their secrets, keep alive his will to power –
waving of plumes, the spread of lies,
mimicry of love and humility.

Oak

An arrival – your grandmother's dresser,
bare, dismembered, flung on a coal lorry –
you recognised as the sentinel

in her Russell Street parlour, the proud display
of willow-patterned plates, remembering
the polished drawer knobs snug in your palms

when you searched for chocolate drops,
and found pencilled letters from the Front
laid to rest in the folds of her best laced linen.

Reassembled in the garden workshop,
the dresser stood like a despoiled universe,
its warped shelves stained by gall ink,

chronicler of hunger, ailing babies, father home
from the pit, scrubbed pink over the tin bath,
his son Dan hammering copper sculptures,

practising his tenor pitch – daily lives
we scraped away with Dowlais grime to buff
and wax the freshened wood. We dressed

shelves with plates, filled drawers with cutlery,
jugs with holly and red berries, draped garlands
of mistletoe and birthday lights.

The dresser settled in, quiet, complaisant.
In time, it hosted familiar visitors: moth
caterpillars, spider mites and wood lice.

When we noticed root heave all along
the skirting boards, wood knots birthing bees,
bats hanging from brass hooks,

you called in our local carpenter, renowned
for making furniture into trees.

The Wasp Catcher

Beside the humming bougainvillea,
I watched wasps hover, dart into flowers.

Some lifted off over our heads to the sea,
like scattered chaff, pieces of light.

A moment passed. I'd wanted to say
something remarkable, but hesitated –

because words, at variance with my thoughts,
danced between us like fireflies. I listened

to your lies with incredulity, smothered
them with fragrance, the way bees

swarm interlopers invading the hive.
A tic in the corner of my eye, and I caught

a glass globe swinging on wire, hooked
to your balcony, wasps like knots of fur

trapped inside – heavy-bellied bees, knife-winged,
buzzed in fury, drowned in honey.

I turned to the pleating of sands below, fish
invisible but for their grey shadows on patrol

like hawk moths with closed wings. I heard
your sweet nothings, but no longer listened –

in the absence of moon, stars slashed
into the ribbed vault – only the comfort

of a flower that grows in the dark.

Once

Along the thin line of contraries, the push
and pull of love, when from your eyes
I saw doves with flint beaks and transparent
wings in the tinny light. But it was a small
sparrow that cowered under the brow
of the house as the hawk made a shadow
over the grass, and stars nestled deeper
into their dark vents, leaving the sky
solemn with an impression of something
once said, like your unfolding story about
how you found refuge from the brutal drift
of things – dirt under your foot-soles,
fields slippery with gore, little red apples
with disease.
                But it was as if
you came from heaven to show me how
to keep alive because I was perishable
as wet leaves and we locked hands
and felt our bodies could never be close
enough, and you confessed your life
was like a chapter of knots, *quipu* leading
only to yourself – a loose thread I could stop
from unravelling in the hour before dusk
between the dog and the wolf. I watched you
leave in the mirror – on the table
an empty glass, a scattering of small change.

Unearthed

Year 3021

In her hand, a brooding stillness – a thing
asleep, sheathed in a glassine jacket

tucked inside a coffer made from wood – maybe
ancient pine with amber flame in the grain.

Her discovery conjures a time long ago when
mallow grew around her ancestral home,

windows and doors flung open, skies full
of real birds singing in gushes and trills.

She doesn't know why peeling away the outer
covering she imagines a ghoulish cache –

hawks' gizzards or severed tongues.
Relieved to touch marbled skin, its scent

of pepper, musk, unguents, warming
in her palm alive, she strokes the spine,

its splinter- cracks releasing beads of gold.
And lifting the lid, she meets the gaze

of a single pith eye, flecked like pelts
of wolves or savanna cats. Curious, she coaxes

the frame to fan open, tissue-petals falling.
With no-one to help or explain, she scans

the dark etchings, then holds them to her ear
listening for its voice – but only a whooshing

sound like someone dying, out of breath.
Tenderly, she returns the mystery into the

earth, into the safe hollow of itself.